Jewish Holidays, Jewish Values

Journal

By Rachael Gelfman Schultz and Aliza Zeff

BEHRMAN HOUSE

www.behrmanhouse.com/holidays-values

To the Educator: Please refer to *Jewish Holidays, Jewish Values: Lesson Plan Manual* for complete lesson plans, background information, project ideas, and more.

Visit www.behrmanhouse.com/holidays-values for further resources about the holidays and values in each chapter, including links to videos, games, puzzles, articles, songs, books, and more.

Encourage learners to explore the free *Jewish Holidays, Jewish Values Game Pack*, filled with fun, content-rich games and puzzles to play online or print out.

Designer: Elynn Cohen
Project editor: Dena Neusner
Editorial consultants: Diane Zimmerman, Nathan Weiner
Chapters 1, 2, 5, 8, 10 by Rachael Gelfman Schultz
Chapters 3, 4, 6, 7, 9 by Aliza Zeff

Copyright © 2014 Behrman House, Inc.
Springfield, New Jersey 07081
www.behrmanhouse.com
ISBN 978-0-87441-917-7
Printed in the United States of America

Library of Congress Cataloging-in-Publication Data
Schultz, Rachael Gelfman.
  Jewish holidays, Jewish values : journal / by
Rachael Gelfman Schultz and Aliza Zeff. – Student journal.
    pages cm
ISBN 978-0-87441-917-7
1. Fasts and feasts–Judaism–Study and teaching (Elementary) 2. Jewish
ethics–Study and teaching (Elementary) 3. Jewish way of life–Study and
teaching (Elementary) I. Zeff, Aliza. II. Title.
  BM690.S3178 2014
  296.4'3–dc23
                            2014000809

The publisher gratefully acknowledges the following sources of photographs and graphic images:
(T=Top, B=Bottom, M=Middle, L=Left, R=Right)

Cover: Shutterstock: Sergey Novikov(kids w/globe),79, Designsstock(pen), Sergey Pinaev(menorah), Howard Sandler(grogger), Elynn Cohen(drawings), Bohbeh(paper-front), Monkik(paper- back); iStockphoto: Sarah Bossert(girl w/matzah), dra_schwartz(sederplate). Interior: Beverly Weiss 1,14B; Creative Image 6; Ginny Twersky 21; Richard Lobell 28, 31T, 48T; iStockphoto: 45BR, ruchela 60T, motomeiri 61T, tovfla 63BR, 68B, oksana2010(parsley) 69; Shutterstock: Khazanova 2,3, Vinko93 5, Jianghaistudio 7T, s1001 7B, Pavel L Photo and Video 8T, Adrian Niederhaeuser 8B, FamVeld 9M, Artush 9B, irencik 10T, gdvcom 10B, cute vector 10M, Yulia Glam 11, Bannykh Alexey Vladimirovich 11B, KERIM 12T, RedKoala 12M, GWImages 12B, lenetstan 13T, Roman Sotola13B, boulemon 15T, A1design 15B, Blend Images 16, Sarycheva Olesia 18, ChameleonsEye 19, 62M, oksix 20, carballo 22, BooHoo 23B, 27BR, Matt Ragen 24T, Bijan Roghanchi 24B, Erik Svoboda 25T, wavebreakmedia 25B, Boule 26, mejnak 27T, Nadasazh 27M, Gayvoronskaya_Yana 27BL, CS stock 29(day 1), Pakhnyushcha 29(day2), TT photo 29(day3), Shukaylova Zinaida 29(day4), Mrs_ya 29(bird day 5), Kletr 29(fish day 5), John Bill 29(day 6), Ofri Stern 30, S1001 31L, pavelr 31R, Clare Sieffert 32, Tachawat Klinpakdee 33T, Leah613 35R, Sukpai-boonwat 36 R, G10ck 37 B, Carmen Medlin 37TR, Blend Images 38MR, Monkey Business Images 38BL, 52B, 76B, 78ML, Deborah Kolb 38BR, Oleg Mikhaylov 38 ML, leonello calvetti 39, Lisa F. Young 40, 42 BL, 78MR, BrAt82 42T, Maglara 42BR, David Grigg 43BL, Mny-Jhee44T, Fotokostic 44B, Sergey Novikov 45T, Noam Armonn 47B, Leah613 48B, Norman Pogson 49ML, Jacek Chabraszewski 49BL, 96B Iakov Filimonov 51, Aggie 11 52T, Andriy Markov 52 M, Alex Illi 53, Anastasia Skachko 54, NagyDodo 56, Ron and Joe 57T, Nikitina Olga 57BR, AlexandreNunes 58, mangostock 59, 64M, bilha Golan 61B, blueeyes 63TR, Jukree Boonprasit 64B, StudioSmart 65M, alexmillos 67M, ledokol.ua 69, MGphotos 69B, Maclaud 71B, DanielK90 71T(bread), Elenarts 71T (circle slash), Denis Barbulat 74T, file404 74B, Dawn Shearer-Simonetti 75T, MANDY GODBEHEAR 75B, ledokol.ua 77T, Noam Armonn 77B, spirit of America 78T, Zurijeta 78B, catwalker 80, Monkik 81B, meunierd 82T, Leah613 83B, encikAn86T, irisphoto1 87L, Arkady Mazor87(Herzl, kibbutzim), Vitezslav Halamka 87(Holocaust graphic), majeczka 87R, Alice Kirichenko 88, Nickolay Vinokurov 88ML, SeanPavonePhoto 88MR, 89TR, dnaveh 88BR, diplomedia 89BL, RnDmS 89TL, voddol 89ML, Aleksandar Todorovic 89MR, urfin 90T, Phish Photography 91, Elzbieta Sekowska 93TR, Alex Illi 94,95, Leon Forado 96T; Wikimedia Commons: Dr. Avishai Teicher Pikiwiki Israel 41TL, ariely 41TR, 73BL Israeli Government Press Office 47T, 47M, 49MR, 72T, Library of Congress: Marion S. Trikosko 46 B, Israel Defense Forces 49BR, 73T, Shivat Minim 55, AlfredovicB 60B, Koshy Koshy 64T, Ernest Normand 66L,72B, FEMA Photo Library, Mark Wolfe 66B(charoset, marror), 69, 72T, Guillaume Rouille 73BR, United States Holocaust Museum 81, Piotr Biega a 82B, Daniel Ullrich, Threedots 84B, Carl Pietzner 85B, 92; Francine Keery 23T; Israel Images/ Israel Talby 17; Yad Vashem The Holocaust Martyrs' and Heroes' Remembrance Authority 46T; Fotolia: Fotolia1 24M; Greensboro *News and Record* 66R; Creative Image 70T; United States Holocaust Memorial Museum, courtesy of William Blye 84T; Jim McMahon 84T; Tom Verniero(Caldwell, NJ) 90B.

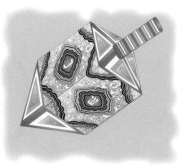

Contents

This journal belongs to:

_____

_____

Shalom!

Perhaps you have some questions…

How can we learn Jewish values from our holiday traditions?

What Jewish values guide us as we celebrate holidays and every day?

Why is this important to me?

The answers are all around you. You can find them in your community, in your friends, and most importantly, inside yourself. This book will help you do just that.

Here's where you get to try out new holiday experiences and discover the meanings behind them. You can imagine yourself in ancient times or facing modern-day dilemmas. You can seize the chance to eat, sing, debate, create, play, draw, and build the connections between our Jewish traditions and your life.

It all starts here. It all starts with you. Are you ready?

The Jewish Year

Why do Jewish holidays seem to fall on different days every year? It's because we're keeping track of two different calendars! Jewish holidays are based on the Hebrew calendar, which follows the cycles of the moon. But the secular calendar that we use every day (also called the Gregorian calendar) is based on the Earth's rotation around the sun. These calendars don't match up exactly, and so dates on the Hebrew calendar don't match up with dates on the secular calendar.

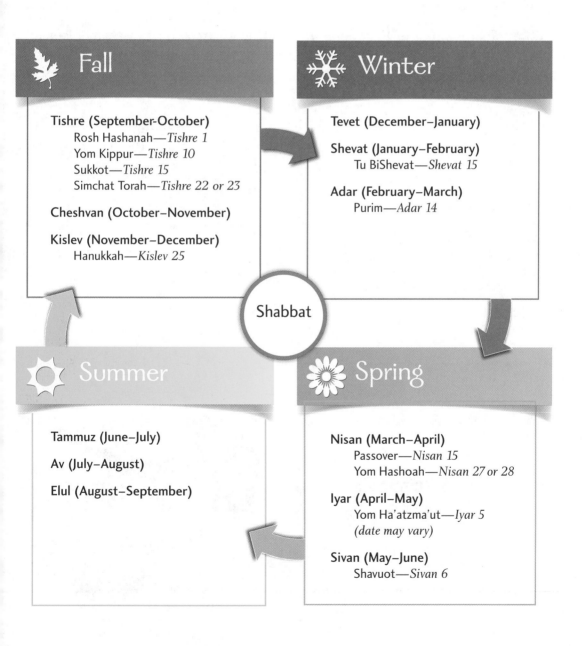

Fall

Tishre (September–October)
Rosh Hashanah—*Tishre 1*
Yom Kippur—*Tishre 10*
Sukkot—*Tishre 15*
Simchat Torah—*Tishre 22 or 23*

Cheshvan (October–November)

Kislev (November–December)
Hanukkah—*Kislev 25*

Winter

Tevet (December–January)

Shevat (January–February)
Tu BiShevat—*Shevat 15*

Adar (February–March)
Purim—*Adar 14*

Shabbat

Summer

Tammuz (June–July)

Av (July–August)

Elul (August–September)

Spring

Nisan (March–April)
Passover—*Nisan 15*
Yom Hashoah—*Nisan 27 or 28*

Iyar (April–May)
Yom Ha'atzma'ut—*Iyar 5*
(date may vary)

Sivan (May–June)
Shavuot—*Sivan 6*

THE HIGH HOLIDAYS

Returning to Our Best Selves • *Teshuvah*

"Wake up," the sound of the shofar tells us on Rosh Hashanah and Yom Kippur.

The shofar reminds us to pay attention to who we are and how we can become our best selves—kinder, more helpful, and more generous. The High Holidays are a time to look closely at our lives and to think deeply about what changes we can make.

Write a short prayer below about how you would like to act in the coming year. You can say this prayer while you listen to the sound of the shofar.

This year, help me to _____

_____

Remind me to _____

_____

_____

Inspire me to _____

_____

We say this blessing when we hear the shofar:

בָּרוּךְ אַתָּה, יְיָ אֱלֹהֵינוּ, מֶלֶךְ הָעוֹלָם, אֲשֶׁר קִדְּשָׁנוּ בְּמִצְוֹתָיו וְצִוָּנוּ לִשְׁמֹעַ קוֹל שׁוֹפָר.

Praised are You, Adonai our God, Ruler of the world, who makes us holy with commandments and commands us to hear the sound of the shofar. (from the *Machzor*, High Holidays prayer book)

Rosh Hashanah Seder

Rosh Hashanah is the Jewish New Year. It is sometimes called the birthday of the world, because according to tradition it is the day that God finished creating the world. We eat apples and honey to represent our wish for a sweet new year. Jewish families of Sephardic (Spanish and Mediterranean) descent hold a festive meal called a Rosh Hashanah seder, at which a number of different foods are eaten to represent our hopes for the New Year. What foods represent your wishes for the coming year?

FOOD	My Wish for the New Year
Apples and Honey 	I wish for a new year that is as sweet as apples and honey.

DID YOU KNOW ? We eat round challah on Rosh Hashanah to represent the circle of life and the cycle of each year.

Tashlich

On Rosh Hashanah afternoon, we symbolically throw away our mistakes or bad choices from the previous year by casting small pieces of bread into a stream or other body of water. This tradition is called *tashlich*, meaning "cast away."

What are some examples of bad choices you made last year that you wish you could throw away to make a fresh beginning? Think about times that you said or did something to hurt someone else or yourself. Write your mistakes on small slips of paper, then rip them up to symbolically cast them away.

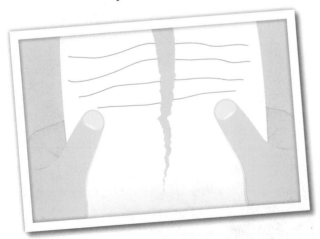

Some people say the following biblical verse when they throw away their sins (bad choices):

And cast into the depths of the seas all of our sins.
(Micah 7:19)

וְתַשְׁלִיךְ בִּמְצֻלוֹת יָם כָּל-חַטֹּאתָם.

What would you do?

Your best friend, Matt, asks whether he can borrow your bike, and you agree. When he returns it you notice that the headlight is broken. You immediately get angry: "How could you break my headlight?! Some friend you are!"

"I didn't break it," Matt says. "It was already like that."

You respond, "You're lying. The last time I rode my bike the headlight was fine. I can't be friends with a liar!"

Matt answers, "Well if you think I am a liar, I don't want to be your friend either!"

The two of you don't speak for several weeks. You really miss Matt and you've always been able to trust him. But it's hard to admit your mistake and apologize. What do you do?

I would _____

because _____

Asking Forgiveness

During the High Holiday season, we ask forgiveness from people we may have hurt during the year.

I will ask forgiveness from _____

_____

_____

for _____

_____

_____

I plan to say _____

_____

_____

Now go ahead and do it! Right now, or when you're at home, find a quiet place to talk. Afterward, think about how it felt.

Right before I asked forgiveness, I felt . . .
☐ nervous   ☐ hopeful   ☐ afraid   ☐ confused   ☐ other _____

Right after I asked forgiveness, I felt . . .
☐ relieved   ☐ happy   ☐ excited   ☐ proud   ☐ other _____

Now think about a time when someone asked you for forgiveness.

When I forgave someone, I felt . . .
☐ relieved   ☐ happy
☐ free   ☐ proud
☐ other _____

Jonah in the Fish's Belly

On Yom Kippur afternoon at synagogue, we read from the book of Jonah in the Bible. It describes how God tells the prophet Jonah to warn the people of the evil city of Nineveh to change their ways. Instead, Jonah runs away, boards a boat, and is tossed overboard during a storm at sea and swallowed by a big fish. Inside the fish's belly, Jonah prays to God for forgiveness and promises he will deliver the warning. The fish spits him out, and he goes to Nineveh, where he persuades the people to change their ways.

What do you think inspired Jonah to change his mind and do the right thing?

Making Meaning תְּשׁוּבָה

Teshuvah is a mitzvah, a commandment from the Torah. It is a Hebrew word that means returning to our best selves, or "repentance."

Jonah was inspired to do *teshuvah* inside the fish's belly. What inspires you to do *teshuvah?* Maybe it is talking with someone you trust, or seeing how you hurt someone, or knowing in your heart that something isn't right. Draw an image of whatever inspires you to do *teshuvah* in the space inside the fish's belly.

Fasting

On Yom Kippur, many Jews fast; we do not eat or drink all day, from sundown to sundown. We may spend the day at synagogue, where fasting helps us focus on our prayers for forgiveness and on doing *teshuvah*. Children who have not yet reached bar or bat mitzvah age are not expected to fast, but you can still choose to give up something on Yom Kippur in order to focus on the day's meaning.

This Yom Kippur, I think I will give up . . .

☐ breakfast or lunch
☐ snacks
☐ a favorite game or sport
☐ television
☐ computer games
☐ comic books
☐ other: _____

I think this will help me reflect on the meaning of the day because

_____

_____

_____

_____

Kol Nidrei

The Yom Kippur evening service begins with a declaration called Kol Nidrei (All Vows), in which we announce our intention to cancel any promises to God that we are not able to keep:

> All vows and oaths, all promises and obligations we make to God between this Yom Kippur and the next—may we take them back if we should forget to do them, and may we be forgiven for them. (from *Kol Nidrei*)

Why do you think we say this? What have you promised this year that you wish you could take back?

I said _____

_____

_____

I wish I could take it back because _____

_____

_____

TRY THIS

Make a Teshuvah Contract.

Brainstorm with your class ways that you can help each other do *teshuvah* this year. Make a list of things that you will work on together, reminding each other to actually do them.

_____   _____

_____   _____

_____   _____

Chapter 2

SUKKOT

Humility • *Anavah*

Gratitude • *Hakarot Hatov*

Imagine what it would be like to wander in the desert for forty years without a real home.

> You shall live in *sukkot* seven days…in order that future generations may know that I made the Israelite people live in *sukkot* when I brought them out of the land of Egypt…. (Leviticus 23:42-43)

The Torah tells us to leave our comfortable homes for a week in order to live in a sukkah (a simple hut that is open to the elements). Even though most of us today do not actually live in the sukkah, synagogues and some families build a sukkah and eat festive meals inside. This helps us remember that our ancestors lived in *sukkot* when they were wandering in the desert.

We say this blessing when we enter the sukkah:

Praised are You, Adonai our God, Ruler of the world, who makes us holy with commandments and commands us to sit in the sukkah.

בָּרוּךְ אַתָּה, יְיָ אֱלֹהֵינוּ, מֶלֶךְ
הָעוֹלָם, אֲשֶׁר קִדְּשָׁנוּ
בְּמִצְוֹתָיו וְצִוָּנוּ לֵישֵׁב בַּסֻּכָּה.

How might living in a sukkah make you feel about your home?

My home is a place where I can _____

_____

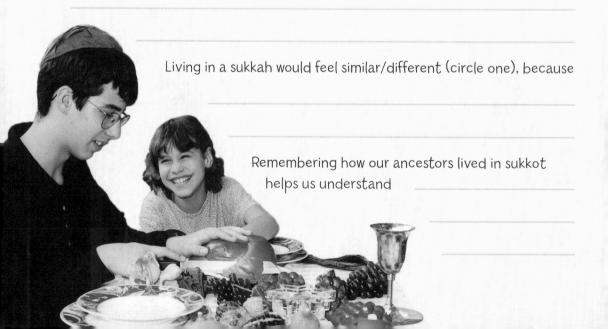

Living in a sukkah would feel similar/different (circle one), because _____

_____

Remembering how our ancestors lived in sukkot helps us understand _____

_____

My Sukkah

Imagine that you are going to spend the week in your very own sukkah that you designed. Draw the design for your sukkah here, and include inside it the basic things that you need to be healthy and reasonably comfortable for the week. Think about what is most important to you, and how you can live more simply and humbly. What do you choose to put inside your sukkah? What do you choose *not* to include? Why?

DID YOU KNOW?

There are certain rules for building a sukkah: the roof must be made out of branches or other cut plants (called s'chach); the roof must be open enough that you can see the stars through it at night; and the sukkah must have at least three walls.

Anavah is the Hebrew word for "humility," being modest and not overly proud. Living in a sukkah teaches us *anavah* by helping us see that our possessions don't make us who we are. It helps us focus on the things that are most important in our lives. How can you show more *anavah* in your life?

I behave with anavah when I _____

_____

_____

Sometimes it is difficult to behave with anavah because _____

_____

_____

_____

What would you do?

Imagine that you are very excited because you scored a 100 on a test that you studied really hard for, with some help from your older brother. You are with a group of friends, and everyone is discussing what they got on the test. What do you say or do? Why? Act out this situation with a partner, trying out different roles. Be prepared to explain how your actions demonstrate *anavah.* Then make up your own situations to demonstrate *anavah,* and act them out.

Personality Quiz: Humility & Gratitude

Our ancestors lived in *sukkot* in their fields during the harvest time.

1. After lots of hard work training, you finally make the basketball team. Do you:
   (a) Congratulate yourself for all your hard work.
   (b) Remind yourself that now you have to work harder than ever to help your team.
   (c) Tell your coaches, parents, and friends how grateful you are for their help.

2. Your mom buys you the cool shoes you've been wanting for a long time. Do you:
   (a) Imagine how great you'll look when you are wearing them.
   (b) Tell your mom she really shouldn't have spent all this money on you.
   (c) Give your mom a big hug and say, "Thanks so much!"

3. You lose the student council elections after putting your heart and soul into the campaign. Do you:
   (a) Reassure yourself that you did your best and ran a great campaign.
   (b) Try to learn what you could have done better during the campaign.
   (c) Focus on how lucky you are to have other activities you enjoy.

4. Sukkot is also an agricultural holiday, on which the ancient Israelites celebrated the harvest. If you were an ancient Israelite, would you:
   (a) Celebrate your success by hosting a festive meal and serving beautiful crops from your fields.
   (b) Analyze and learn from what went well and what didn't go well during this harvest season.
   (c) Bring a sacrifice thanking God for your good harvest.

What are the pros and cons of pride, humility, and gratitude?

If your answers were mostly . . .

(a): You are proud of yourself and make sure to celebrate your own accomplishments.
(b): You are humble. You are quick to recognize the mistakes you make and to learn from them so you can do better next time.
(c): You are grateful for those who have helped get you to where you are today, and you are quick to express your thanks.

The Jewish Thanksgiving

The ancient Israelites waved the four species (what we call the *lulav* and *etrog*) on Sukkot as a way of giving thanks to God for the completed harvest. The Torah says:

> . . . On the fifteenth day of the seventh month, when you have gathered in the fruits of the land, you shall keep the feast of Adonai for seven days....On the first day you shall take the product of citrus trees, branches of palm trees, boughs of myrtle trees, and willows of the brook, and you shall rejoice before Adonai your God seven days. (Leviticus 23:39-40)

How is the biblical celebration of Sukkot similar to or different from the American celebration of Thanksgiving? Write some words that describe these holidays in the circles provided.

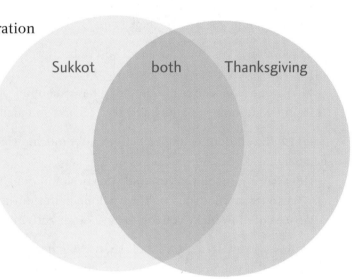

Sukkot   both   Thanksgiving

How Do We Shake the Lulav and Etrog?

Praised are You, Adonai our God, Ruler of the world, who makes us holy with commandments and commands us to lift up the *lulav*.

בָּרוּךְ אַתָּה, יְיָ אֱלֹהֵינוּ, מֶלֶךְ הָעוֹלָם,
אֲשֶׁר קִדְּשָׁנוּ בְּמִצְוֹתָיו וְצִוָּנוּ עַל
נְטִילַת לוּלָב.

Think of a time you worked hard at something and were successful. Now shake the *lulav* and *etrog*, and express your thanks to God, as our ancestors did in biblical times. Shake it in six directions: to the front, right, back, left, up, and down.

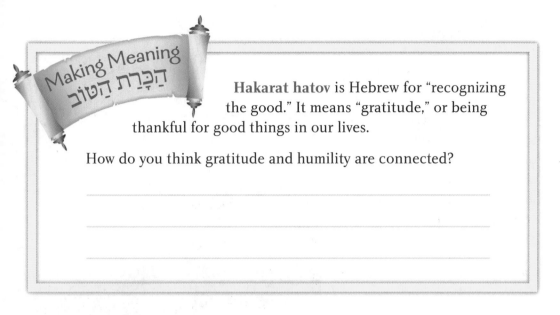

Making Meaning
הַכָּרַת הַטוֹב

Hakarat hatov is Hebrew for "recognizing the good." It means "gratitude," or being thankful for good things in our lives.

How do you think gratitude and humility are connected?

_____

_____

_____

Ushpizin: Inviting Guests

One way to show gratitude for what we have is to share with others. On Sukkot, some Jews invite guests into their sukkah to share a festive meal. *Ushpizin*, the Aramaic word for guests, refers to the traditional idea that a different guest from Jewish history comes to visit us in the sukkah each night of Sukkot, starting on the first night with our ancestor Abraham and ending with King David.

Imagine that you could invite a guest from Jewish history or tradition to the sukkah. Who would you invite? What would you talk about? Act it out with a friend.

I would invite _____

because _____

_____

We would talk about _____

_____

_____

My Hallel

I give thanks to You, for You have answered me… (Psalms 118:21)

Another way that Jews celebrate Sukkot is by saying Hallel, a collection of psalms praising God for all the good that God does for us. Write and/or draw your own Hallel prayer to give thanks for the blessings in your life.

I give thanks for:

Chapter 3

SIMCHAT TORAH

Rejoicing · *Simchah*

What makes you want to celebrate?

On Simchat Torah, we are actually commanded to rejoice with the Torah. We sing and dance with the Torah to celebrate our joy in it as the source of our traditions, laws, values, and stories. What else makes you want to sing, dance, or celebrate in another way?

I want to celebrate when _____

_____

_____

I celebrate important moments with my family because _____

_____

_____

I think we celebrate the Torah because _____

_____

_____

_____

_____

Simchah is the Hebrew word for "joy" or "happiness." On Simchat Torah, we express our joy in a public way, but *simchah* can be felt and expressed in many ways. What are some ways you show *simchah*?

☐ laugh   ☐ smile

☐ cheer   ☐ sing

☐ hug   ☐ dance

☐ jump up and down

☐ other: _____

What Does Simchat Torah Mean?

Design an app button or book cover based on the two words of the holiday's name: *simchah* and *Torah*. How will you include these two ideas in your design? Which one will be the focus? Be ready to explain your drawing in class.

How Do We Celebrate?

On Simchat Torah, we come together in the synagogue for a service that is full of celebration. Which of the following activities do you like best? Grab a partner and lead your friends—or your class, or your family—in the celebration.

DANCING

On Simchat Torah, we do *hakafot*, seven rounds of singing and dancing with the Torah.

If you were holding the Torah and leading the congregation in the *hakafah*, what would you do?

Plan this with a friend, and then lead others in a *hakafah*.

SINGING

During the holiday celebration, the congregation sings many songs related to the Torah and rejoicing.

Learn the following song or make up your own and teach it to a friend.

שִׂשׂוּ וְשִׂמְחוּ בְּשִׂמְחַת תּוֹרָה וּתְנוּ כָּבוֹד לַתּוֹרָה

Rejoice and be happy on Simchat Torah, and let us honor the Torah.

READING

On Simchat Torah, we celebrate the completion of an entire cycle of reading the Torah, and we begin the cycle again with the story of Creation.

What is your favorite Torah story? Act it out or retell it with friends.

Visit www.behrmanhouse.com/holidays-values to learn how to dance a horah and to hear the song "Sisu V'simchu."

Investigating the Torah

Take a close look at a Torah scroll, if you have the opportunity to visit the sanctuary. Can you identify these objects on a real Torah? Draw lines from the descriptions to the corresponding items in all three of the pictures.

1. crown or *rimonim*
(decorative items placed on top of the *atzei chayim*)

2. breastplate
(decorative metal plate)

3. mantle
(cloth cover)

4. *yad*
(pointer used by the Torah reader to keep his or her place while reading)

5. *atzei chayim*
(wooden rollers)

6. binder or belt
(cloth band that holds the Torah closed)

7. parchment
(the material on which a Torah scroll is written, made from the skin of a kosher animal)

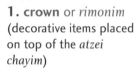

I think we dress the Torah with these objects because

_____

_____

_____

_____

What would you do?

You and your friend have decided to enter a short story competition. Your friend asks you to help with the editing of her story, since you are such a good writer. You agree to help her. When the results of the contest are announced, you are disappointed that you didn't win, even though you wrote a great story. Then you find out that your friend has won the competition. How do you react?

At first, I feel _____

_____

_____

_____

But when I stop and think about my friend's feelings, I

_____

_____

_____

When I congratulate my friend, I celebrate these values (check those that apply):

☐ friendship　　☐ hard work　　☐ loyalty

☐ simchah　　　 ☐ other _____

Simchah in Our Lives

On Simchat Torah, we are commanded to rejoice. And in the book of Psalms, it says:

> Worship God with joy,
> Go before God in song.
> (Psalms 100:2)

I think "worship God with joy" means _____

_____

_____

I live joyfully when I _____

_____

_____

I like to share my joy with others because _____

_____

_____

It can be hard for me to share my happiness with others when _____

_____

_____

DID YOU KNOW ?

An annual Simchat Torah party in the streets of New York City draws thousands of Jewish people. What values do you think they are demonstrating by holding this public celebration?

What Makes You Happy?

On a note card, write down one thing that makes you happy. The catch? It should not be a material thing, like a Wii or your favorite jeans. Sit in a circle and pass your notes around the group. As you receive each note, decide whether the thing written there brings you happiness, too. If so, put a check mark on it. If not, just pass it on.

What does it mean if there are a lot of check marks on your note? What if there aren't?

What does your choice say about what's important in your life?

TRY THIS

Plan a Torah party to share with another class, or with your friends and family at home. With a partner, choose appropriate music, food, decorations, and activities to celebrate our joy in the Torah.

Chapter 4

SHABBAT

Holy Time and Space · *Bein Kodesh L'Chol*
Peace · *Shalom*

On the seventh day...God rested. (Genesis 2:2)

You may have heard this phrase from the Torah, but what does it really mean? Resting on Shabbat isn't just about getting extra sleep. It can mean sharing peaceful times with family and friends, saying Shabbat blessings, slowing down and letting our minds wander, going to synagogue, or hearing stories of our families and our ancestors. How does our rest on Shabbat help make Shabbat holy? How does it help bring peace into the world?

Write an acrostic poem about Shabbat, in which each line starts with a letter from the word *peace*.

P _____

E _____

A _____

C _____

E _____

_____

And on the Seventh Day...

The idea of observing Shabbat comes from the Torah. In the book of Genesis, the creation of the world took six days. Then...

> God blessed the seventh day and declared it holy; because on it God rested from all the work of creation that God had done. (Genesis 2:3)

How would you represent the seventh day in a picture? Draw your idea in the seventh box. Then explain how it represents the idea of rest.

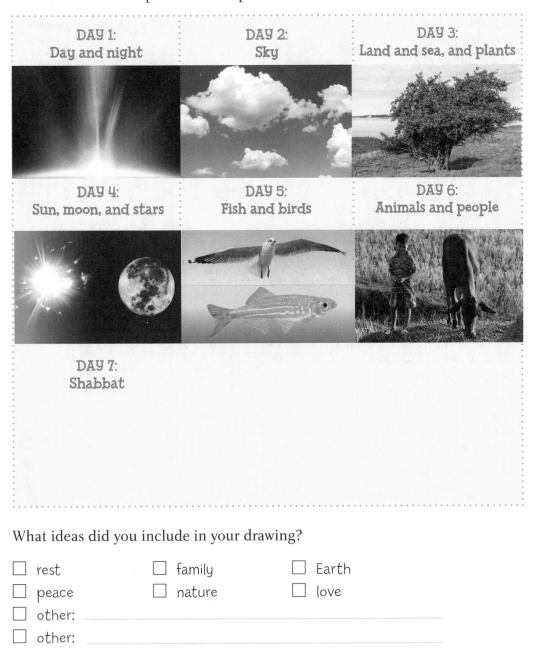

DAY 1:
Day and night

DAY 2:
Sky

DAY 3:
Land and sea, and plants

DAY 4:
Sun, moon, and stars

DAY 5:
Fish and birds

DAY 6:
Animals and people

DAY 7:
Shabbat

What ideas did you include in your drawing?

- ☐ rest
- ☐ peace
- ☐ other: _____
- ☐ other: _____
- ☐ family
- ☐ nature
- ☐ Earth
- ☐ love

Welcoming Shabbat

Where does the tradition of lighting candles to welcome Shabbat come from?

There is a midrash (a story) that says that Shabbat candles were lit by the very first Jews, starting with Abraham's wife Sarah. The candles lasted all week, casting a brightness and shine on everything in their home. Sarah passed this tradition on to all the generations that followed.

Does your family have its own Shabbat traditions? Share the story of your family's customs, or of a special Kiddush cup or candlesticks that may have been passed down from earlier generations.

Light candles together, or act out the lighting of candles, and practice the blessing.

Praised are You, Adonai our God, Ruler of the world, who makes us holy with commandments and commands us to light the Shabbat candles.

בָּרוּךְ אַתָּה, יְיָ אֱלֹהֵינוּ, מֶלֶךְ הָעוֹלָם, אֲשֶׁר קִדְּשָׁנוּ בְּמִצְוֹתָיו וְצִוָּנוּ לְהַדְלִיק נֵר שֶׁל שַׁבָּת.

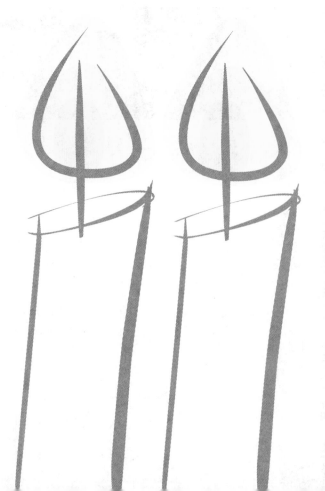

Sit quietly for a minute and watch the flames dancing and flickering. Think about the following questions, and write any words or phrases that come to mind inside the candlesticks:

- What feeling do you get when the candles are lit?

- What does candlelight make you think of?

- What are you grateful for on Shabbat?

How does your family welcome Shabbat?

Kiddush, the blessing over wine or grape juice, and Hamotzi, the blessing over bread, are essential parts of the Shabbat meal. Together with the class, say these blessings, sip the grape juice, and taste the challah.

Praised are You, Adonai our God, Ruler of the world, who creates the fruit of the vine.

בָּרוּךְ אַתָּה, יְיָ אֱלֹהֵינוּ, מֶלֶךְ הָעוֹלָם, בּוֹרֵא פְּרִי הַגָּפֶן.

Praised are You, Adonai our God, Ruler of the world, who brings forth bread from the earth.

בָּרוּךְ אַתָּה, יְיָ אֱלֹהֵינוּ, מֶלֶךְ הָעוֹלָם, הַמּוֹצִיא לֶחֶם מִן הָאָרֶץ.

Going to Synagogue

Shabbat services are held in the synagogue on Friday night and Saturday. On Shabbat morning we read the *parashah*, the Torah portion for the week, and the *Haftarah*, the accompanying Bible portion from one of the books of the Prophets. We sing and recite prayers together with our community.

At synagogue, I participate by _____

Silently, I say _____

I listen to _____

I like it when _____

The sentences below are all mixed up. The objects in column 1 are all found in the synagogue sanctuary. Draw a line from each object to the words that describe it in column 2. Then continue your line to the correct words in columns 3, 4, and 5 to complete the sentence. The first one has been done for you.

Start here: (1)	(2)	(3)	(4)	(5)
The *bimah* is...	the Ark, or cabinet,...	where the Torah reading takes place...	and it's always lit...	so that the whole congregation can see.
The reader's desk (or lectern) is...	the raised platform...	that hangs over the Ark...	and it's in the front or center of the room...	to represent God's eternal presence.
The *Aron Hakodesh* is...	the table on the *bimah*...	on which the Torah is placed when it is read...	and it's raised above the ground...	to face the holy city of Jerusalem.
The *Ner Tamid* is...	the eternal lamp...	in which the Torah scrolls are kept...	and it's usually located on the eastern wall...	so that the whole congregation can see.

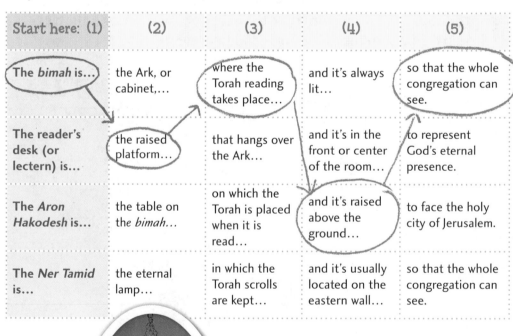

The *Ner Tamid* is never extinguished or turned off.

Making a Transition

Our Friday night traditions help us mark the transition from the regular week to Shabbat. Make a list of some other times in your day or in your life when you mark a transition, switching from one activity to another or even from one stage of life to another. What do you do in order to acknowledge the change? Some examples are filled in to help you get started.

Transition	What Do I Do To Mark the Change?
The end of the day	Put on pajamas; turn out the lights.
A birthday	Make a wish and blow out birthday candles.

Why do you think we mark transitions? _____

_____

_____

Bein kodesh l'chol is Hebrew for
"between the holy and the everyday."
What are some ways we shift from the holiness
(*kodesh*) of Shabbat to the everyday (*l'chol*)?

Have a Model Havdalah Service!

The phrase *bein kodesh l'chol* is found in the Havdalah service, which helps
us mark the transition between Shabbat and the rest of the week. Try to
identify all five senses at work as we model the service for the close of
Shabbat together:

First we light the braided Havdalah candle (with permission). Then, lift the
cup of grape juice. Look at it, smell it, but don't taste it yet. We say Kiddush
to mark the beginning of Shabbat and also the end. Together we say:

Praised are You, Adonai our God, Ruler of the world, who creates the fruit of the vine.	בָּרוּךְ אַתָּה, יְיָ אֱלֹהֵינוּ, מֶלֶךְ הָעוֹלָם, בּוֹרֵא פְּרִי הַגָּפֶן.

Smell the spices to bring the sweet
scent of Shabbat into the week.

Praised are You, Adonai our God, Ruler of the world, who creates various kinds of spices.	בָּרוּךְ אַתָּה, יְיָ אֱלֹהֵינוּ, מֶלֶךְ הָעוֹלָם, בּוֹרֵא מִינֵי בְשָׂמִים.

The flames of the braided candle
remind us of the separation of
darkness from light, the holy from
the everyday. We say:

Praised are You, Adonai our God, Ruler of the world, who creates the fiery lights.	בָּרוּךְ אַתָּה, יְיָ אֱלֹהֵינוּ, מֶלֶךְ הָעוֹלָם, בּוֹרֵא מְאוֹרֵי הָאֵשׁ.

Then we say the blessing thanking God for separating the holy from the everyday. Listen for the Hebrew words you learned that mark that transition. Lift the cup of grape juice again, and say:

Praised are You, Adonai our God, Ruler of the world, who separates the holy from the everyday, light from darkness, Israel from the other nations, the seventh day from the six days of work. Praised are You, Adonai, who separates the holy from the everyday.

בָּרוּךְ אַתָּה, יְיָ אֱלֹהֵינוּ,
מֶלֶךְ הָעוֹלָם, הַמַּבְדִּיל
בֵּין קֹדֶשׁ לְחוֹל, בֵּין אוֹר
לְחשֶׁךְ, בֵּין יִשְׂרָאֵל
לָעַמִּים, בֵּין יוֹם הַשְּׁבִיעִי
לְשֵׁשֶׁת יְמֵי הַמַּעֲשֶׂה.
בָּרוּךְ אַתָּה, יְיָ, הַמַּבְדִּיל
בֵּין קֹדֶשׁ לְחוֹל.

Finally, we sip the grape juice and extinguish the candle in what remains. Listen carefully to the sizzle of the flame as it is extinguished.

Holy Time and Space

Shabbat helps us separate *bein kodesh l'chol*, between the holy and the everyday. But what does the word "holy" mean? What is holy time? What is holy space? Write some words that describe what these ideas mean to you in the circles below. In the overlapping area, write words that apply to both holy time and holy space.

Holy time　　both　　Holy Space

Shabbat helps create holy time and space for me by

_____

_____

_____

_____

Bein Kodesh L'chol Challenge

What can you do to make Shabbat more meaningful this week? Write a list of ideas. It can be anything that makes Shabbat a restful, peaceful, or holy time and space.

I will _____

I can _____

I plan to _____

I might _____

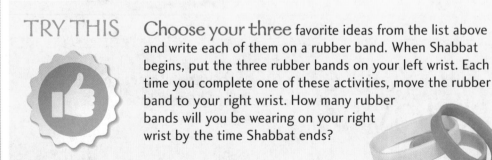

TRY THIS Choose your three favorite ideas from the list above and write each of them on a rubber band. When Shabbat begins, put the three rubber bands on your left wrist. Each time you complete one of these activities, move the rubber band to your right wrist. How many rubber bands will you be wearing on your right wrist by the time Shabbat ends?

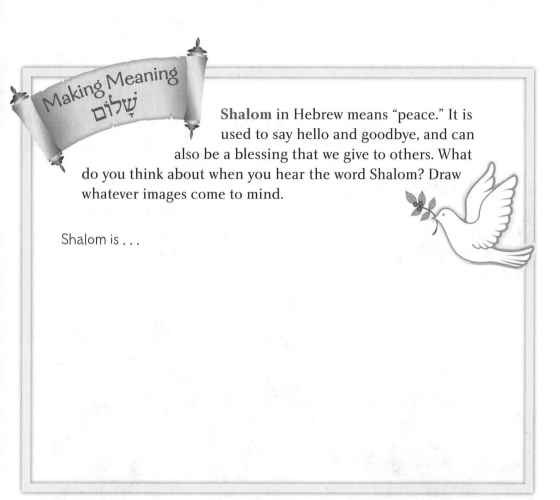

Shalom in Hebrew means "peace." It is used to say hello and goodbye, and can also be a blessing that we give to others. What do you think about when you hear the word Shalom? Draw whatever images come to mind.

Shalom is . . .

Shalom Inside

The word *shalom* is related to the Hebrew word *shaleim*, שָׁלֵם which means "whole" or "complete." Feeling peaceful or complete inside is something we can aim for anytime, and especially on Shabbat, our day of rest.

What can you do before or during Shabbat to prepare yourself for a feeling of shalom deep inside? Draw or write your ideas in the sections of the peace sign.

Values in Action:

Sh'lom Bayit

Part of observing Shabbat is creating a peaceful time and space. We aim to do this at the synagogue, with friends, and especially in our homes. We value *sh'lom bayit*, "peace in the home," not just on Shabbat, but all the time. With a partner, choose one or more of the images below, and together make up a story about *sh'lom bayit* or tell about a time when you have experienced *sh'lom bayit* in your home.

Sim Shalom

Listen to a recording of Sim Shalom,
or sing it together. You can find a link at
www.behrmanhouse.com/holidays-values.
Then read the prayer in English:

Grant peace, goodness, and blessing,
graciousness, and kindness, and mercy
upon us and upon all Your people Israel.

Bless us, our Parent, all of us as one, with the light
of Your presence, for with the light of Your presence,
Adonai our God, you gave us the Torah of life, and a love
of kindness, and righteousness, and blessing, and mercy, and
life, and peace.

May it be good in Your eyes to bless Your people Israel and all peoples
at all times and at every hour with Your peace.

Praised are You, Adonai, who blesses Your people Israel with peace.

Circle the ingredients for peace that you see in the prayer above.

I think a peaceful world needs _____

_____

_____

_____

_____

I can create more peace in my life, my home, and the world by _____

_____

_____

_____

_____

_____

Chapter 5

HANUKKAH

Courage • *Gevurah*

Who are your heroes?

On Hanukkah, we remember how the Maccabees stood up and fought against the powerful Syrian army for the right to practice their religion. We celebrate the Maccabees as heroes for their courageous acts. What makes someone a hero? What are some different ways to show courage?

I think _____ is a hero

because _____

_____

_____

_____

People show courage when _____

_____

_____

_____

I feel courageous when I _____

_____

_____

_____

 +

What Is the Miracle of Hanukkah?

Long ago, the land of Israel was ruled by the Syrians. Their king, Antiochus, filled the Holy Temple with idols and ordered the Jews to worship Greek gods, as the Syrians did.

But the Jews rebelled. The Maccabees, a small group of fighters without training or weapons, fought back and defeated the powerful Syrian army.

After the Maccabees won, they wanted to restore and rededicate the Temple. They found enough oil to light the holy Menorah only for one day. But the oil lasted eight days, long enough for them to be able to make more oil.

Which miracle that we celebrate on Hanukkah do you think is more important? List the reasons for each view, then have a debate with a partner.

Miracle of the oil	Miracle of the military victory

Think about how fighting the Syrians and lighting the Menorah both showed courage. Which act do you think required more courage?

Human Menorah

The Menorah in the Temple had seven branches, but the *hanukkiyah*, the Hanukkah menorah, has eight branches to remember the miracle of the oil that lasted for eight days.

Create a human menorah with the students in your class. Eight students, representing the eight branches of the menorah, sit in a row at the front of the room. Another student represents the ninth candle, the *shamash*. The *shamash* shows how the candles are all lit on the eighth night by tapping the candles on the shoulder one by one from left to right. Each candle stands up when lit. As each candle stands up, that student finishes the following sentence out loud:

I would stand up for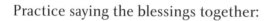

Practice saying the blessings together:

Praised are You, Adonai our God, Ruler of the world, who makes us holy with commandments and commands us to light the Hanukkah candles.

בָּרוּךְ אַתָּה, יְיָ אֱלֹהֵינוּ, מֶלֶךְ הָעוֹלָם, אֲשֶׁר קִדְּשָׁנוּ בְּמִצְוֹתָיו וְצִוָּנוּ לְהַדְלִיק נֵר שֶׁל חֲנֻכָּה.

Praised are You, Adonai our God, Ruler of the world, who made miracles for our ancestors in those days at this time.

בָּרוּךְ אַתָּה, יְיָ אֱלֹהֵינוּ, מֶלֶךְ הָעוֹלָם, שֶׁעָשָׂה נִסִּים לַאֲבוֹתֵינוּ בַּיָּמִים הָהֵם בַּזְּמַן הַזֶּה.

(This third blessing, the *Shehecheyanu*, is said on the first night of Hanukkah only.)

Praised are You, Adonai our God, Ruler of the world, who has given us life, sustained us, and enabled us to reach this time.

בָּרוּךְ אַתָּה, יְיָ אֱלֹהֵינוּ, מֶלֶךְ הָעוֹלָם, שֶׁהֶחֱיָנוּ, וְקִיְּמָנוּ, וְהִגִּיעָנוּ לַזְּמַן הַזֶּה.

We eat foods fried in oil, such as latkes (potato pancakes) or *sufganiyot* (jelly doughnuts), to remember the miracle of the oil.

Gevurah is the Hebrew word for "courage" or "strength." It comes from the same root letters as the Hebrew word for "hero," *gibor*. What do you think it means to be a *gibor*, גִּבּוֹר and to show courage? Discuss your responses with a friend, and illustrate them together, using images, symbols, or cartoons.

What would you do?

You are the captain of your soccer team, and your biggest game of the season falls on Yom Kippur. You are playing your arch rivals, and the whole team is depending on you. But you always go with your family to the synagogue on Yom Kippur, and last year you even fasted for the first time. Your parents say that they will go to services this year as usual, and they hope you will join them, but you are old enough to make your own decision, and they will respect whatever decision you make. Do you play the game or not? Why?

I would _____

because _____

"Mi Y'maleil"

"Mi Y'maleil" ("Who Can Retell") is a popular
Hanukkah song. Try to sing it in a round!

Mi y'maleil g'vurot Yisrael otan mi yimneh?
Hein b'chol dor yakum hagibor, go'eil ha'am.
Sh'ma! Bayamim haheim baz'man hazeh
Makabi moshi'a ufodeh.Uv'yameinu kol am Yisrael
yitacheid yakum l'higa'eil.

Who can retell the things that befell us,
Who can count them?
In every age, a hero or sage
Came to our aid.

Hark! In days of yore in
Israel's ancient land,
Brave Maccabeus led the faithful band.
And now all Israel must as one arise,
Redeem itself through deed and sacrifice!

According to this song, which miracle
do we celebrate on Hanukkah? Whose
courage are we singing about?

What do you think the last two
lines of the song mean? How can
we follow the Maccabees' example?

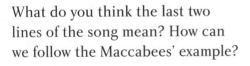

✎ Visit www.behrmanhouse.com/holidays-values for a link to the song.

Values in Action:
"In Every Age, a Hero or Sage"

Who are the heroes in modern times who rose up to save the Jewish people? Choose one of the heroes below, or another one of your choice, and answer the following questions:

- What challenges did this person face?

- How did this person show courage in overcoming these challenges?

- What makes this person a hero?

Find information in books or online at
www.behrmanhouse.com/holidays-values.
Present your answers to the class as a skit,
PowerPoint, song, poem, newspaper article,
or poster.

Oskar Schindler was a German industrialist who saved the lives of over twelve hundred Jews during the Holocaust by employing them in his factory.

Golda Meir helped build the State of Israel and represent it to the rest of the world. She became the first female prime minister of Israel in 1969.

Yoni Netanyahu led Operation Entebbe, the Israeli military operation that rescued more than 100 Jews held hostage by terrorists in Uganda in 1976.

Natan Sharansky (shown far right) fought for the rights of Jews from the Soviet Union to immigrate to Israel. After being imprisoned in Siberia for nine years, he was freed and allowed to immigrate to Israel in 1986, where he became a human rights activist and politician.

Jewish Pride

We light the *hanukkiyah* on Hanukkah and place it in the window of our homes in order to share the miracle of Hanukkah. We declare to everyone who passes by our pride in being Jewish.

I am proud to be Jewish when _____

_____

_____

I show my Jewish pride by _____

_____

Playing Dreidel

When King Antiochus declared that Jews could no longer study Torah, they continued to do so secretly. According to tradition, when a Syrian would approach a secret study group, Jews would pretend they were just playing *dreidel,* a game with a spinning top.

Have you ever had to hide or go against your beliefs?

When _____

_____

_____

I chose to _____

_____

_____

I felt 😁 😦

☐ nervous   ☐ proud   ☐ angry   ☐ confused   ☐ sneaky

☐ scared   ☐ excited   ☐ strong   ☐ other _____

If there's time, play a game of dreidel with your class. Later, you can teach a friend or family member to play as well. Visit www.behrmanhouse.com/holidays-values for directions on how to play dreidel.

The letters on the dreidel stand for the Hebrew phrase נֵס גָּדוֹל הָיָה שָׁם, which means "a great miracle happened there."

Values in Action:

Courage in Our World Today

There are many different ways of showing courage in our world today. Look carefully at the images below. How are these people being courageous? How would you act in these situations?

A girl says no to a cigarette.

Jewish and Arab teachers promote understanding between their communities in Israel.

A girl tells a bully that she doesn't like what he is doing and that he should stop.

Volunteers in Israel's Magen David Adom provide emergency medical services.

Who Is Courageous?

Who is courageous? One who conquers his or her impulse to do evil, as it is written, "One who is slow to anger is better than a hero, and one who rules over his or her spirit [is better] than one who conquers a city." (Pirkei Avot 4:1 commenting on Proverbs 16:32)

According to this teaching, which act shown in the images on the previous page is the most courageous? Why?

TRY THIS

Make a collage of images of courage. You could include images from the Hanukkah story, images of the heroes that you researched, and stories of courage from your own life and from your family members. Try to include many different types of courage in your collage. Plan your collage here.

TU BISHEVAT

Caring for the Environment · *Bal Tashchit*

Happy New Year!?

We usually think of January 1 as New Year's Day, and we celebrate the Jewish New Year on Rosh Hashanah. But did you know there is another new year that we honor? Tu BiShevat is also called "The New Year for the Trees." On this holiday, we celebrate the beginning of a new year of growth for trees by showing our gratitude for all that the natural world gives us.

When I think about nature, I am grateful for _____

_____

_____

because _____

_____

_____

I think Judaism celebrates nature because

_____

_____

_____

_____

_____

The Old Man and the Carob Tree

A long time ago, an old man was busy planting a carob tree as the king rode by. "Old man," the king called out, "how old are you?"

"Seventy years, your majesty," the old man replied.

"How many years will it take for that tree to bear fruit?" asked the king.

"Perhaps seventy years," the man replied.

Mockingly, the king went on. "Do you really expect to ever eat of the fruit of the tree?"

"Of course not," the man said, "but just as I found fruit trees when I was born, I plant trees so that future generations may eat from them."

(Babylonian Talmud, *Ta'anit* 23a)

I can follow the old man's example by _____

_____

_____

I care about future generations because

_____

_____

_____

Why Celebrate Trees?

We celebrate Tu BiShevat, the "birthday of the trees," by tasting fruits and nuts that come from trees, and by learning about and thanking God for the cycles in nature that help trees to grow.

What do trees do for us besides giving us fruit? Fill in additional things that trees provide on the branches and leaves in the illustration.

Which item do you feel is the most important? Why? _____

_____

_____

DID YOU KNOW ?

Israel is one of only two countries in the world that began the twenty-first century with MORE trees than it had 100 years ago. This is due to extensive conservation and planting of trees by the Jewish National Fund, and the donations of Jews from around the world.

Tree Observation

It is sometimes hard to appreciate something
without taking a careful look. Take a few moments to sit
quietly and observe a tree. As you do, think about these questions:

- What does the tree look like? What are its parts? What is its shape?
- Does the tree still have its leaves?
- Does the tree have a smell?
- How is the tree similar to or different from others around it?
- How might this tree be important to other plants, or to people
  or animals?

Now write or draw your observations here.

PUZZLE TIME: Seven Species

The Bible lists seven species of grains and fruits that are special crops of Israel, and that we traditionally eat on Tu BiShevat. Use the clues, or look up the Bible verses, to find the seven species in this puzzle.

Across

4. This fruit has hundreds of tiny red seeds and is said to have inspired the design on the robe of the Temple's high priest (see Exodus 28:33–34).

6. This fruit is usually eaten dried or baked into small cakes. The leaves of this tree are said to have been used to clothe Adam and Eve (see Genesis 3:7).

7. This fruit can be used to make wine. When Moses sent spies into the land of Israel, they brought back bunches of this fruit that were so large they had to be carried on a pole by two men (see Numbers 13:23).

Down

1. This grain is used in hearty soups and other dishes, and is celebrated on Shavuot (see Deuteronomy 8:8).

2. This grain has been used to make challah for more than 2,000 years (see Exodus 34:22).

3. Dates are a sweet, sticky fruit that can be eaten dried or made into date honey. They grow on a date _____ tree (see Exodus 15:27).

5. This green pitted fruit can be eaten or pressed to make oil for cooking or for lighting an oil lamp (see Exodus 27:20).

Bal tashchit means "do not destroy" in Hebrew. This commandment comes straight from the Torah:

> When in your war against a city…you must not destroy its trees, wielding the ax against them. You may eat of them, but you must not cut them down…. Only trees that you know do not yield food may be destroyed…. (Deuteronomy 20:19-20)

Explain this commandment in your own words.

_____

_____

In today's world, we apply the value of *bal tashchit* not only to trees during wartime, but to all of earth's natural resources, including fuel, water, food, and even the air we breathe! Why is this ancient commandment important to remember in our world today?

_____

_____

_____

Deforestation is the process of cutting down a forest and converting the land to another use, such as farming or housing developments.

Bal Tashchit Game

What are some examples of *bal tashchit* in your life? In small groups, take turns drawing a simple object that represents *bal tashchit*—for example, a light switch could represent "turning off the lights to save electricity." The first person to identify the action represented by the drawing gets a point!

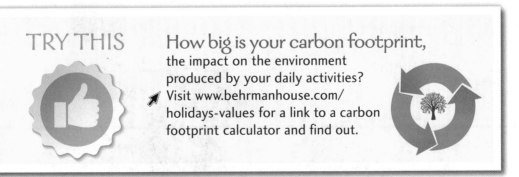

TRY THIS

How big is your carbon footprint, the impact on the environment produced by your daily activities? Visit www.behrmanhouse.com/holidays-values for a link to a carbon footprint calculator and find out.

Making It Happen: A Tu BiShevat Proposal

What can you do to promote *bal tashchit* in your school? With a friend or in small groups, brainstorm ideas for something you can do on Tu BiShevat and throughout the year. Choose one idea and write a letter to the education director, or create a skit, poster, PowerPoint, or even a song. Make notes for your idea here, then get creative!

Bal tashchit teaches us that _____

_____

Our bal tashchit idea for the school is _____

_____

To do this idea, first we will _____

_____

Then we will _____

_____

Tu BiShevat is a great time to do this because _____

_____

Acting on Bal Tashchit

Our rabbis taught:

> You are not required to complete the task, but you are not free to avoid it.
> *(Pirkei Avot 2:21)*

What does this mean for us, in terms of acting on *bal tashchit*?

_____

_____

_____

_____

_____

Chapter 7

PURIM

Justice • *Tzedek*
Giving • *Tzedakah*

How does it feel to make a difference in the world?

On Purim, we learn how Esther and Mordecai saved the Jews of Shushan by standing up to Haman, despite the risks to their own lives. We celebrate the victory of the Jewish people by wearing costumes and making noise, and by giving gifts to friends and tzedakah to those in need.

Think about a time when you made a difference by standing up for something you believed in or helping a person in need. What did you do? How did it feel?

I made a difference by _____

_____

_____

I did it because _____

_____

_____

_____

Doing this felt _____

_____

_____

_____

VOLUNTEER

TZEDAKAH

The Purim Story

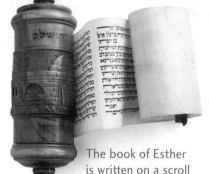

On Purim, we read *Megillat Esther*, the scroll that tells the story of Purim. Don't forget to make a lot of noise to drown out Haman's name!

The book of Esther is written on a scroll called a *megillah*.

Hundreds of years ago, King Ahasuerus of Persia hosted a party that lasted an entire week! Drunk with wine, the king ordered his wife Vashti to show off her beauty for all to admire. But Vashti refused. Angry that she had disobeyed his orders, Ahasuerus sent Vashti away.

Now Ahasuerus needed a new queen. He held a pageant for all the young women of the kingdom and chose the beautiful Esther. The fact that she was Jewish remained a secret.

Meanwhile, the king's new adviser, Haman, commanded all the people to bow down to him. But Esther's uncle, Mordecai, refused. Haman was so angry, that he plotted to destroy the Jewish people. He convinced the king to issue a royal decree: On the thirteenth day of the month of Adar, the people of Persia would rise up against the Jews and kill them all.

Mordecai urged Esther to speak to the king and tell him that she was Jewish. Esther was afraid. It was a crime punishable by death to appear before the king when he had not called. But she had no choice; she had to take the risk.

Before Esther visited the king, she asked Mordecai and all the other Jews of Shushan to fast and pray for her. Then she went before the king and invited him and Haman to a banquet. She told the king that she was a Jew and that Haman wanted to kill her and all her people. The king was outraged! He ordered Haman to be hung on the gallows that he had built for Mordecai. The Jews were saved!

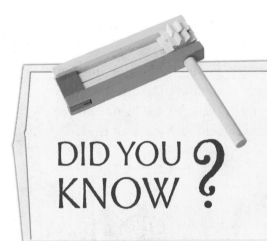

DID YOU KNOW ?

There are **4** *mitzvot* that we are commanded to do on Purim: read the *megillah*, give gifts of food to our friends and family, give to the poor, and have a festive meal.

Imagine you are Esther or Mordecai in this story. How did you feel when you stood up for your beliefs?

☐ Frightened ☐ Nervous ☐ Brave ☐ Clever
☐ Excited ☐ Other _____

Have you ever taken a big risk to stand up for something?

_____
_____
_____
_____

What did you do? _____

_____
_____
_____

Tzedakah means giving to those in need. In the Torah we are commanded to give because it is the just and right thing to do. Tzedakah includes giving money, clothing, food, and time.

The Mitzvah of Giving

On Purim, we celebrate our good fortune by giving *matanot la'evyonim*, gifts to the poor, and *mishlo'ach manot*, gifts of food to our friends and family. In fact, it is a mitzvah, a commandment, to give, as it says in the *megillah*:

> "They were to observe them as days of feasting and merrymaking, and as an occasion for sending gifts to one another and presents to the poor. (Esther 9:22)

How does giving gifts help strengthen our community?

_____

_____

_____

_____

We all like to get nice things, but how does it feel to give?
And what are the reasons we give?

I give gifts to friends and family because _____

_____

When I give gifts, I feel: 🙂 🙁

- ☐ happy ☐ proud ☐ cheerful
- ☐ silly ☐ excited ☐ _____

I give tzedakah, help those in need, because

_____

_____

When I do tzedakah, I feel: 🙂 🙁

- ☐ nervous ☐ concerned ☐ hopeful
- ☐ proud ☐ connected ☐ _____

Hamantashen can be filled with all sorts of things, from the traditional poppy seeds, prunes, or apricots, to all kinds of jam, nuts, and even chocolate chips. What's your favorite flavor?

Do you think we should still give even if it doesn't make us feel good?
Why or why not?

_____

_____

_____

TRY THIS

Prepare mishlo'ach manot, bags or baskets of food to give to friends or family members. Include a card in each gift stating three reasons why you are giving it. And don't forget the *hamantashen*!

Values in Action:

Tzedakah around the World

Choose one of the images on this page and explain to a partner this religion's attitude about giving to those in need. Why do you think tzedakah is a value that is found in all cultures?

In Islam, giving to those in need is called *zakat*, or "purification," because it is said to purify a person's heart from becoming greedy. Performing *zakat* is a reminder to Muslims that everything they have really belongs to God.

Christians believe that **charity** is an expression of love of God, self, and others, and that it is their responsibility to help others. During the season leading up to Easter, called Lent, Christians make an extra effort to help the poor and their neighbors in need.

Buddhists practice *dana*, a form of charity given without expecting anything in return. It can involve giving money, time, knowledge, or anything that can benefit others. Buddhists believe that giving in this way helps reduce greed.

Making Meaning צֶדֶק

In Hebrew, **tzedek** means "justice", or seeking what is fair and right for ourselves and others. Notice that the word *tzedek* looks and sounds a lot like *tzedakah:* צְדָקָה

Which Hebrew letters do these two words have in common?

_____

Why do you think these two words are related?

_____

_____

_____

_____

_____

_____

DID YOU KNOW ?

צ ד ק

Most Hebrew words are made up of three basic letters, called root letters. Related words can be made from those three letters by adding different letters to the beginning or end of a word.

Values in Action:

Pursuing Justice

Choose one of the pictures below. Explain how the value of *tzedek* is shown.

The people in this picture are standing up for tzedek by

_____

_____

I think they are feeling _____

_____

_____

If I were in their place, I would _____

_____

_____

Esther and Haman
before Ahasuerus
(Ernest Normand, 1888)

A peaceful protest
at a "Whites only"
restaurant, 1960

Rebuilding homes
destroyed by
Hurricane
Katrina in 2005

Tzedek Today

With a partner, brainstorm injustices that exist today. This can include anything from homelessness to a student being treated unfairly at school. The Torah says, *"Tzedek, tzedek tirdof,"* which means "Justice, justice you shall pursue." (Deuteronomy 16:20)

We all have a responsibility to stand up to injustices. List or draw three injustices in the world today and ideas for what *you* can do to help make it right.

Injustice	Possible ways to make it right

How are these actions similar to the way Esther and Mordechai stood up to injustice?

_____

_____

_____

Chapter 8

PASSOVER

Loving the Stranger • *Ahavat Hager*

In every generation, each of us must see ourselves as if we personally went out of Egypt. (from the Haggadah)

We read these words every year at the Passover seder, but what do they really mean? During Passover, we remember the ancient Israelites, slaves who suffered under hard work and cruel masters until they finally took courageous steps to freedom. Imagine you are one of the Israelite slaves who left Egypt. Tell your story.

As a slave in Egypt, I had to _____

_____

_____

Finally, Pharaoh said we could leave! Then _____

_____

_____

After we crossed the Sea of Reeds, I felt. . .

- ☐ hopeful
- ☐ joyful
- ☐ afraid
- ☐ excited
- ☐ safe
- ☐ proud
- ☐ awed
- ☐ grateful
- ☐ strong
- ☐ tired
- ☐ nervous
- ☐ sad
- ☐ happy
- ☐ angry
- ☐ confused

because _____

_____

_____

_____

A Taste of the Exodus

Food can hold a lot of meaning. On Passover, the foods we eat remind us of how the Israelites were slaves in Egypt. Taste each of the foods on the chart below, paying close attention to texture and taste. Then think about why we eat this food at the seder. Your answers might or might not be the same as those in the haggadah. Be creative!

FOOD	How I felt while eating this food	This reminds me of the slaves in Egypt because . . .
Karpas dipped in salt water		
Matzah		
Maror		
Charoset		

The seder plate includes:

1. a bitter herb (*maror*)
2. a roasted egg (*beitzah*)
3. a roasted shank bone (*z'roa*)
4. a second bitter vegetable (*chazeret*)
5. a mix of fruit and nuts (*charoset*)
6. parsley (*karpas*)

Visit www.behrmanhouse.com/holidays-values for a link to the Passover blessings.

Four Questions

Another way that we learn about and remember the Exodus is by asking questions. Each seder starts with the Mah Nishtanah, the Four Questions.

Why is this night different from all other nights?

מַה נִּשְׁתַּנָּה הַלַּיְלָה הַזֶּה מִכָּל הַלֵּילוֹת?

1. On all other nights we eat leavened products and matzah; on this night only matzah.

שֶׁבְּכָל הַלֵּילוֹת אָנוּ אוֹכְלִין חָמֵץ וּמַצָּה,
הַלַּיְלָה הַזֶּה כֻּלּוֹ מַצָּה.

2. On all other nights we eat all vegetables; on this night only bitter herbs.

שֶׁבְּכָל הַלֵּילוֹת אָנוּ אוֹכְלִין שְׁאָר
יְרָקוֹת, הַלַּיְלָה הַזֶּה מָרוֹר.

3. On all other nights, we don't dip our food even once; on this night we dip twice.

שֶׁבְּכָל הַלֵּילוֹת אֵין אָנוּ מַטְבִּילִין,
אֲפִילוּ פַּעַם אֶחָת, הַלַּיְלָה הַזֶּה
שְׁתֵּי פְעָמִים.

4. On all other nights we eat sitting or reclining, on this night we all recline.

שֶׁבְּכָל הַלֵּילוֹת אָנוּ אוֹכְלִין בֵּין
יוֹשְׁבִין וּבֵין מְסֻבִּין, הַלַּיְלָה הַזֶּה
כֻּלָּנוּ מְסֻבִּין.

We are encouraged to ask our own questions at the seder, too. Imagine that you could go back in time and talk to an Israelite slave in Egypt. What Four Questions would you ask?

1. _____

2. _____

3. _____

4. _____

During Passover, we don't eat *chameitz* (leavened products), such as bread, cookies, or cakes.

DID YOU KNOW?

The number 4 appears many times during the Passover seder. There are the **Four** Questions, **four** children, **four** cups of wine or grape juice, and **four** different words used for the redemption from Egypt.

Values in Action:

In Every Generation

The Exodus from Egypt is not just a long-ago historical event. In every generation, Jews are redeemed—freed or saved from danger. Choose one of the examples below from Jewish history, and imagine that you were there. What was life like for you? How did it feel to be redeemed? Act out your experience for your classmates.

Ethiopian Jews made *aliyah* to Israel, with the largest group coming in Operation Solomon in 1991.

The Purim story tells how the Jews were saved from death at the hands of Haman in Shushan.

Gilad Shalit, an Israeli soldier, was released in 2011 after being held in captivity in Gaza for more than five years.

After years of protests by Jews around the world, Jews were finally allowed to leave the Soviet Union in the 1980s.

The Hanukkah story describes how the Maccabees successfully rebelled against the Syrians in 165 BCE.

Find more information on these topics in books or online at www.behrmanhouse.com/holidays-values.

73

Avadim Hayinu

This Passover song celebrates our journey from slavery to freedom.

> *Avadim hayinu l'Faroh b'Mitzrayim,*
> *atah b'nei chorin.*
> We were slaves to Pharaoh in
> Egypt—now we are free.
> (from the Haggadah)

Why do you think it uses the word *we* instead of *they*?

Loving the Stranger

The Torah tells us one way we can act as if we had been freed from Egypt:

> When a stranger lives with you in your land, do not mistreat him.
> The stranger living with you must be treated as one of your
> citizens. Love him as yourself, for you were strangers in Egypt.
> I am Adonai your God. (Leviticus 19:33-34)

In this quote from the Torah, a "stranger" means an outsider, someone who might need help or protection. It does not mean someone we don't know (like when our parents tell us, "Don't talk to strangers!").

I think "love the stranger as yourself" means _____

_____

_____

Remembering what it was like to be a slave
in Egypt helps us love the stranger because

_____

_____

_____

The kids in your school always pick on Becky, a girl in your class. They make fun of her accent, her clothes, and even her nervous laugh. Every day at lunch, Becky sits by herself, reading a book. You always sit with your four best friends. When you suggest inviting Becky to join you, your friends say, "That would be awful. She's so annoying! Besides, then people would start making fun of *us*."

What would you do? Why?

I would _____

_____

because _____

_____

Now imagine you are Becky. How do you feel during lunch?

I feel _____

_____

I wish _____

_____

The great Jewish scholar Sforno says that loving someone as yourself means developing empathy for that person—imagining what you would feel like in their place and acting with compassion toward them:

> "Love for your neighbor what you would love for yourself if you were in his place." (Sforno, commentary on Leviticus 19:18).

What would Sforno say you should do in the situation described above?

Making Meaning
אַהֲבַת הַגֵּר

Ahavat hager is a mitzvah, a commandment from the Torah. It means "love the stranger" in Hebrew. A "stranger" might be a new neighbor, a recent immigrant who doesn't speak English, or someone at school who seems to be alone.

Think about someone who might be considered a stranger in your life, and draw your responses to the prompts below.

This is what it would feel like to be in that person's shoes . . .

One thing I could do to make that person's life a little better is. . .

Matzah, the Bread of Affliction

At the beginning of the seder, we hold up the matzah and invite all who are needy to come celebrate Passover with us:

> "This is the bread of affliction [poverty] that our fathers ate in the land of Egypt. Whoever is hungry, let him come and eat; whoever is in need, let him come and join in the celebration of Passover."
> (from the Haggadah)

Take a bite of matzah. How many words can you think of to describe its look and taste?

_____ _____ _____

_____ _____ _____

_____ _____ _____

How might eating matzah, the "bread of affliction" (poverty), remind us to care for the needy?

_____

_____

_____

_____

_____

Values in Action:

Loving the Stranger

In today's world, it's not always easy or even safe to invite a needy stranger to our family seder. What other ways can we help the stranger this Passover, or anytime? For each photograph below, imagine what it feels like to be in this person's shoes—to have empathy for them—and describe what actions you might take to help them.

Supporting sports competitions, such as the Special Olympics, for people with disabilities

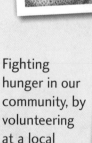

Teaching English to new immigrants, such as through an ESL (English as a Second Language) program

Fighting hunger in our community, by volunteering at a local food kitchen

Caring for the elderly, by spending time with people who are alone, or bringing them food or medicine

What Can We Do to Help?

YOU can make a difference for the strangers in our world. Choose a volunteer or fundraising project that you might like to do by yourself or with a partner to help people in need. It can be inspired by one of the projects on the previous page or something completely different. After you have chosen your project, fill out the planning chart below, one step at a time.

My project is _____

	WHAT I (or we) will do	HOW to do it	WHEN it will be done
Step #1			
Step #2			
Step #3			

Share something about your project at your family seder. Be prepared to explain how the project is connected to the Passover seder and to the mitzvah of *ahavat ha-ger,* loving the stranger.

YOM HASHOAH AND YOM HA'ATZMA'UT

Remembrance • *Zikaron*
Jewish Community • *K'lal Yisrael*

"In spite of everything, I still believe that people are really good at heart." (Anne Frank)

Anne Frank, who died in the Holocaust at age 15, spent the last two years of her life hiding in an attic in Amsterdam. Every day, she and her family feared being found and killed by the Nazis. Yet, she wrote this surprising sentence in her diary. How could she have believed this, given her situation?

Imagine you could write her a letter. What would you say?

Dear Anne Frank, _____

_____

_____

_____

_____

_____

Yom Hashoah: Why We Remember the Holocaust

Yom Hashoah, Holocaust Remembrance Day, is a day to remember a terrible disaster that happened to the Jewish people. The Holocaust refers to the systematic murder of approximately six million Jews by the Nazis. They were led by a man named Adolf Hitler, who wanted Germany to rule the world and who blamed the Jewish people for Germany's problems.

Warsaw Ghetto, Poland, 1943

This is not ancient history—it happened during World War II, probably around the time your grandparents were young. Yom Hashoah is observed by Jews all over the world in many ways—by talking to survivors, reading stories, learning about ancestors who died, lighting memorial candles, or saying prayers.

Watch *Why We Remember the Holocaust*, a video from the United States Holocaust Memorial Museum that gives an introduction to the Holocaust. (Visit www.behrmanhouse.com/holidays-values for a link to the video.)

Write or draw your reactions to the video here.

Lessons from the Torah

"Carefully guard yourself and your soul, so that you do not forget the things you saw with your own eyes, and so that they do not fade from your mind as long as you live. And make them known to your children and to your children's children."
(Deuteronomy 4:9)

Why do you think it's important to remember events such as the Holocaust?

Sachsenhausen Concentration Camp, memorial in stained glass

How can we remember the Holocaust if we didn't see it "with our own eyes" and if it happened before we were born?

DID YOU KNOW ?

Janusz Korczak

During the Holocaust, many people risked their lives to fight back and help others. Jews in the Warsaw Ghetto and other places fought the Nazis with homemade weapons. Secret newspapers allowed groups to organize and help those in danger. More than 27,000 non-Jews helped save Jews from the Nazis by hiding them or helping them to escape.

Zikaron is the Hebrew word for "remembrance." How do you remember an important moment from the past or a special person who is not alive anymore?

I remember this person or moment: _____

_____

_____

Here's how I remember: _____

_____

_____

It is important to remember because _____

_____

_____

With a partner or in a small group, list actions we can take to remember the Holocaust.

_____

_____

_____

_____

Many Jews light a *yahrtzeit* candle as a way of remembering someone who has died. We also light *yahrtzeit* candles on Yom Hashoah, in memory of all those who perished during the Holocaust.

Art Connection

During the Holocaust, some people used art as a way to bring hope and strength to their lives. People played music, wrote stories and poetry, drew pictures, and even painted. How do you express yourself artistically? Here or on a separate paper, design a poster, write a poem, or draw a picture that conveys our responsibility to one another to always remember the Holocaust.

Drawing by a Jewish prisoner at Le Vernet transit camp in France. The writing says, "We have been robbed of all our possessions, yet we maintain our belief in God and trust that this great God will allow us to look calmly into the future."

DID YOU KNOW?

During World War II, Jews living in countries controlled by the Nazis were forced to wear yellow stars on their clothing so that they could be easily identified as Jews.

A Modern Jewish State

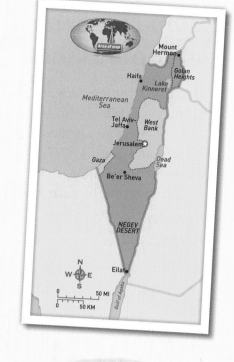

"If you will it, it is no dream."
(Theodor Herzl)

In the 1890s, Theodor Herzl, a Jewish jour-
nalist from Vienna, led the early movement to
establish a modern Jewish state in the land of
Israel. Many people endured hardships and
sacrifice while working to build a country
where Jews would always be welcome. Herzl
died long before his dream came true, but in
1948, soon after the Holocaust, Israel gained
independence, providing a home to many
thousands of Jews who had survived.

What would you say in a letter to Herzl?
What would you want him to know about
his dream?

Dear Theodor Herzl, _____

_____

_____

_____

_____

_____

_____

_____

_____

_____

Yom Ha'atzma'ut: Israel's Independence Day

On Israel's Independence Day, Yom Ha'atzma'ut, we celebrate the modern State of Israel and its accomplishments, history, and culture. Using the key words below, write a definition for each of the following terms. Be sure to explain the difference between them.

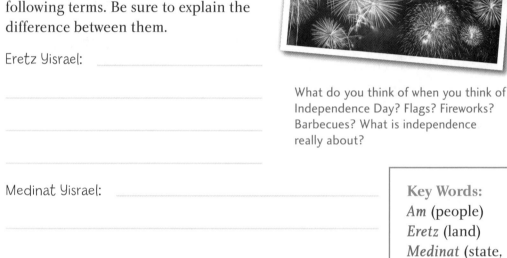

Eretz Yisrael: _____

_____

_____

_____

What do you think of when you think of Independence Day? Flags? Fireworks? Barbecues? What is independence really about?

Medinat Yisrael: _____

_____

_____

Am Yisrael: _____

_____

Key Words:
Am (people)
Eretz (land)
Medinat (state, country)
Yisrael (Israel)

Making Meaning כְּלַל יִשְׂרָאֵל

K'lal Yisrael is a Hebrew phrase that means "all of Israel." It expresses our connection to fellow Jews all over the world.

On Yom Ha'atzma'ut, we celebrate our connection with the land and people of Israel. Israel means many things to us: it is the land of our ancestors and our ancient history; it is a nation that offers a home to Jews from anywhere in the world; it is a place where the majority of the people are Jewish, and Jewish holidays are national holidays. In what ways do you feel connected to *k'lal Yisrael*?

Building a Jewish State

Many important events led up to Israel's independence as a Jewish state.
Draw lines matching the facts in the colored panels below to the dates on
the timeline where they belong.

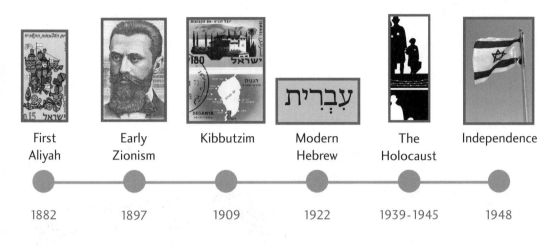

First Aliyah	Early Zionism	Kibbutzim	Modern Hebrew	The Holocaust	Independence
1882	1897	1909	1922	1939-1945	1948

Eliezer Ben-Yehuda leads a movement to transform ancient Hebrew into a modern language. Hebrew becomes the official language of the Jews in Palestine, helping Jews from all over the world talk to each other.

The first kibbutz (plural, *kibbutzim*) is founded in Palestine. A kibbutz is a community in which property and responsibilities are shared by all.

Millions of European Jews lose their lives at the hands of the Nazis. Afterward the survivors need a place to go, adding urgency to the Zionists' goal of creating a Jewish state.

The first wave of Jews moves to the land of Israel (then called Palestine) to escape growing violence against Jews throughout Europe. (The Second Aliyah begins in 1904.)

David Ben-Gurion, the first prime minister of Israel, announces the establishment of the State of Israel, a place that all Jewish people can call home.

Theodor Herzl promotes Zionism, the idea of founding a Jewish state in the land of Israel. He convenes the First Zionist Congress in Switzerland.

How do these events demonstrate k'lal Yisrael? _____

Celebrate Israel!

Israel is a land of contrasts, where you'll find wide open expanses of desert, skyscrapers and nightlife, and ancient holy sites such as the Kotel, the Western Wall. Israelis celebrate Yom Ha'atzma'ut with parades, singing, dancing, hikes, and picnics. Israeli flags are everywhere.

On Yom Ha'atzma'ut, we celebrate the value of *k'lal Yisrael*, our shared community with Jews in Israel and around the world, by tasting Israeli foods, listening to Israeli music, and learning about Israel.

Salt formations in the Dead Sea

A *shuk*, or open-air market

TRY THIS

Try something new from Israel and write about it here:

I tasted _____

I listened to _____

I tried _____

I saw _____

Israel Scouts on their way to summer camp

Ethiopian Jewish women celebrate Sigd

The Western Wall and Dome of the Rock in Jerusalem

The city of Tiberias and Lake Kinneret (also called the Sea of Galilee)

Musicians performing on Yom Ha'atzma'ut in Jerusalem

DID YOU KNOW ?

Kibbeh

Modern Israel is made up of Jewish people from all over the world, creating a diverse community and symbolizing *k'lal Yisrael* even inside this tiny country. Jews from Iraq brought kibbeh, pockets of dough filled with ground meat and spices. Ethiopian Jews brought their own holiday, Sigd. More than a million Jews in Israel today trace their roots to Russia.

Chapter 10

SHAVUOT

Learning from the Torah • *Talmud Torah*

What is the best gift you ever received?

On Shavuot, we celebrate a wonderful gift, the Torah. In our prayers, Shavuot is called *Z'man Matan Torateinu* (the Time of the Giving of Our Torah), because according to our tradition God gave the Torah to the Jewish people on this day. *Matan* comes from the same Hebrew word as *matanah*, "gift."

The Torah gives us the stories of our ancestors and important guidelines for how to live—how to be the best Jews and the best people we can be. The Jewish values we have learned about in this book all come from the Torah.

List some ways in which the Torah is a gift:

I am thankful for the gift of Torah because

My Ten Commandments

On Shavuot, the Ten Commandments are read at synagogue as part of our celebration of the gift of the Torah. Many see the Ten Commandments as the most important list of dos and don'ts in all of Judaism—they reflect some of our most important Jewish values. Read the Ten Commandments, from Exodus chapter 20. Then write *your own* Ten Commandments—the most important dos and don'ts that you live by.

1. _____

2. _____

3. _____

4. _____

5. _____

6. _____

7. _____

8. _____

9. _____

10. _____

Giving from Our Harvest

On Shavuot, we also celebrate the beginning of harvest time, when the ancient Israelites gathered the first fruits from their fields. The Israelites were commanded to leave some of their harvest in the fields for the poor to come take:

> When you reap [cut and gather] the harvest of your land, you shall not reap all the way to the edges of your field or gather the gleanings [what is dropped or left in the field] of your harvest. You shall not pick your vineyard bare, nor gather the fallen fruit of your vineyard; you shall leave them for the poor and the stranger, for I am Adonai your God. (Leviticus 19:9-10)

Ruth and Boaz, by Gustave Dore, 1866

In the Book of Ruth, which we read on Shavuot, Boaz leaves some of the harvest behind so that Ruth and her mother-in-law will have food to eat.

Why is this mitzvah so important that it's included in the Torah?

_____

_____

_____

Most of us are no longer farmers. What can we do to fulfill the spirit of this mitzvah in our lives today?

_____

_____

_____

_____

Dairy on Shavuot

On Shavuot, we eat dairy treats, such as blintzes or cheesecake. One reason for this custom is that the Torah is compared to milk and honey. Why do you think the Torah is compared to something that is healthy and sweet?

_____

_____

_____

_____

Making Meaning תַּלְמוּד תּוֹרָה

Talmud Torah is a mitzvah, a commandment from the Torah. In Hebrew, it means "learning Torah." The rabbis tell us that we learn Torah in order to know how to act:

Rabbi Shimon, son of Rabbi Gamli'el, said…It is not the study of Torah that is the essential thing; it is the doing of it. (*Pirkei Avot* 1:17)

I have learned from the Torah to _____

_____

_____

The Torah guides me when _____

_____

_____

_____

Torah Values

The values that we have learned about over the course of the year all come from the Bible, which includes the Torah and the books of the Prophets and Writings.

Read the verses and match each one with the Jewish value that it teaches us. Write the sentence number and the English meaning of each value in the leaf.

anavah
_____
_____

gevurah
__6__
Courage

teshuvah
_____
_____

1 "And cast into the depths of the seas all of our sins." (Micah 7:19)

2. Love the stranger as yourself, for you were strangers in Egypt. (Leviticus 19:33-34)

3. "…When you have gathered in the fruits of the land, you shall keep the feast of Adonai seven days…" (Leviticus 23:39-40)

4. "When in your war against a city…you must not destroy its trees, wielding the ax against them." (Deuteronomy 20:19)

5. "Moses was a very humble person, more so than any other person on earth." (Numbers 12:3)

6. "One who is slow to anger is better than a hero, and one who rules over his or her spirit [is better] than one who conquers a city." (Proverbs 16:32)

7. "Never stop speaking about this book of Torah. Recite it day and night, so that you may observe faithfully all that is written in it." (Joshua 1:8)

8. "Worship God with joy, go before God in song." (Psalms 100:2)

9. "You will distinguish between the holy and the everyday…" (Leviticus 10:10)

10. "Justice, justice, you shall pursue…" (Deuteronomy 16:20)

11. "For I know God, and he will command his children to perform deeds of righteousness…" (Genesis 18:19)

12. "Carefully guard yourself and your soul, so that you do not forget the things you saw with your own eyes…" (Deuteronomy 4:9)

13. "And I will grant peace to the land, and you will lie down and none will make you afraid." (Leviticus 26:6)

14. "Wherever you go, I will go; and where you lodge, I will lodge; your people shall be my people, and your God my God." (Ruth 1:16)

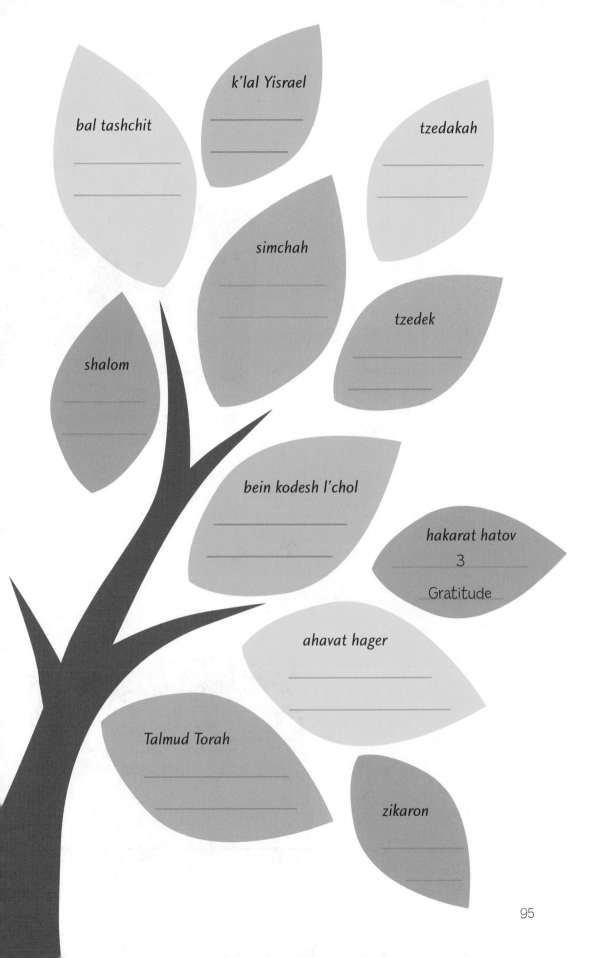

bal tashchit

k'lal Yisrael

tzedakah

simchah

tzedek

shalom

bein kodesh l'chol

hakarat hatov

3

Gratitude

ahavat hager

Talmud Torah

zikaron

95

DEVELOPING AN ACTION PLAN

Jewish values are rooted in the Torah and in the stories and lessons of our Jewish holidays and traditions. What Jewish values do you want to build into your life?

Fill in the steps below with your ideas for trying new holiday traditions and bringing Jewish values even more deeply into your life. Try to be as specific as possible.

In Sephardic Jewish communities, Torah scrolls are kept in hard cases.

This week, I will _____

_____

_____

This month, I will _____

_____

_____

This year, I will _____

_____

_____

_____

_____

_____

_____